Fun Days!

Katacha Díaz

Photographs by Ken O'Donoghue

Rigby

I pet my cat on Sunday.
I like my cat!

Sunday	Monday	Tuesday	Wednesday	Thursday	Friday	Saturday
X						

9

I play in the pool
on Thursday.
I like to play!

☀ DAYS OF THE WEEK ☀						
Sunday	Monday	Tuesday	Wednesday	Thursday	Friday	Saturday
				X		

I ride my bike on Friday.
I like my bike!

☀ DAYS OF THE WEEK ☀						
Sunday	Monday	Tuesday	Wednesday	Thursday	Friday	Saturday
					X	

I plant flowers
on Saturday.
I like my flowers!

	DAYS OF THE WEEK					
Sunday	Monday	Tuesday	Wednesday	Thursday	Friday	Saturday
						X

I have fun
seven days
a week!

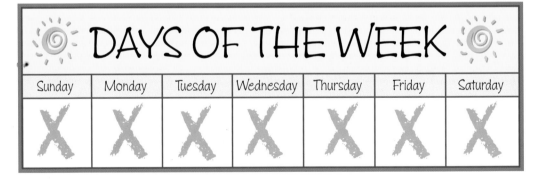

☀	DAYS OF THE WEEK	☀

Sunday	Monday	Tuesday	Wednesday	Thursday	Friday	Saturday
X	X	X	X	X	X	X

3

I play with my friends
on Tuesday.
I like my friends!

Sunday	Monday	Tuesday	Wednesday	Thursday	Friday	Saturday
		X				

DAYS OF THE WEEK

I sing and dance
on Wednesday.
I like to dance!

DAYS OF THE WEEK						
Sunday	Monday	Tuesday	Wednesday	Thursday	Friday	Saturday
			X			